COME, FOLL(

SELECTED POEMS

BY

Sheila Jacob

Dedications and acknowledgments

I owe an immense debt of gratitude to Fr.John Daley, Parish Priest of St.Joseph's Parish, Leicester, who suggested that I publish the bulk of my poems in this one collection. Since 2004,when I first submitted work to the Watermead Apostolate at St.Joseph's, his enthusiasm, and prayerful support, has never wavered. A number of these poems were first published as Wordscapes for Watermead, arranged and printed by Alison Kennedy and illustrated with great beauty and empathy by artist Lynn Tooher.Thank you, Lynn and Alison.

Particular thanks also to Dorothy, my first Ignatian Prayer Guide, who gave me a postcard of a Sieger Koder painting to meditate on." Peter's Feet" was the outcome, which Dorothy read, and ordered, "Keep writing!"

The following people have helped me more than they know by their prayer, appreciative response and inspirational presence:

Meg, Clare and Ash, my terrific grown-up children.

Sheilagh, my dear friend and spiritual mentor, and her fellowship of ecumenical prayer groups in Ballina, Co.Mayo; Pat and John; Michele; Thelma; Betty M; Hanni and Bob; Fr.John A.Woolley and Ros; Pam; Gerry; Elizabeth Roberts; Margaret Martin; Vicki Cameron; Fr Pat Sayles; James and Debbie Crean; the Sisters of La Sainte Union and Srs. Maureen and Catherine of St.Joseph's of Chambery in Wrexham;Sister Margaret Barry

the Carmelites of Dolgellau and the Poor Clare Collettine Community of Ty Mam Duw, Hawarden.

May the Lord bless you all mightily.

This whole venture would have been impossible without the love, loyalty, understanding, friendship (and technical expertise in Microsoft Word and cut& paste!) of my husband Roger.This book is for him, with deepest gratitude and love.

Finally, I give thanks and praise to our Lord and Saviour Jesus Christ, whose Spirit has worked within me to produce these poems. To Him be the glory.

Wrexham, N.E.Wales;
October 2007

"Man of Light" was first published in "Africa" missionary magazine.

The theology in "Ben" is strongly influenced by Fr.John Saward's marvellous work, "Redeemer in the womb".

All Scripture quotations are from The New Jerusalem Bible.

Table Of Contents

Hosea to his unfaithful wife

"But look, I am going to seduce her and lead her into the desert and speak to her heart" Hosea 1; 11

Because in the desert
You will be alone
Except for me.

When you thirst
I will be the stream
You drink from.
When you hunger
My words will be
Manna from heaven.
When you shiver
I will be the fleece
That covers you.

You will have
Nowhere to run to
Because I am
Your hiding place.

I will not spoil you
With rubies
Or silken robes
And you will sit confused;
Wonder how the groom
Can win his bride.

And because
You hang your head
I will tell you.
Because you are afraid
I will speak tenderly
Again and again
Until you lift your face
To mine.

In the silence
Of caves and clefts
You will hear my voice.

In the chafing
Of dust on dry grass
Your heart will grow still.

Then you will see,
Little dove,
That no one
Will ever love you
As I love you.

Peter's Boat

Luke 5:1-11

I dream about it
Most nights, now.

Its storms;
Its anointed stillness.

So when they ask
*"Did you really just
Rise and follow him?"*
I begin at the lake,
Hazy with heat that morning
And me, eager to be home
After we'd trawled all night
And caught nothing.

We left our boats ashore
While we washed the nets.
He was preaching;
(Gathered more followers
Than John ever did.)

Then he was in
My little boat
As though he'd always
Sat there: asked if I'd
Row into the shallows
So the crowd
Could hear him better.

His voice ran pure and clear
Over children, old men.

What did he preach?

I scarcely listened;
Thought how each morning
Would never be the same

Because of this man,
Suddenly Master
Of my boat, my time,
My livelihood....

Put out again, he told us:
Right into the deep.

Some power in his voice
Made me obey
And our nets bulged so much
They began to rip as
We waded and gaped
Like the slithery fish
We humped into creaking boats
Before we stood back,
Startled, confused.

I fell to my knees
Ripe with the smell
Of fish-scales and sin,
My heart naked
Before my Lord.

I let it slip
Into his hands.

Visitation

Luke 1:39-45

I needed to see Elizabeth:
Share in her delight
At the secret
She had hugged
For six long months.

Gentle kinswoman,
Scorned by the world
For her barrenness
But then, when hope
Had almost faded…

I went without delay,
Eager to help,
Be at her side
As she waited
For the birth.

A long journey
Into the hills.

Time to ponder
The angel's visit
And my own miracle.

Time to fret over Joseph
For I had left no word,
Sent no explanation.

I needed Elizabeth
And her quiet counsel;

Weaved through her courtyard,
Called out my greeting.

We hugged, laughed:

Were nudged apart
By the sudden movement
Of her unborn son,
Plump as a pear
Between our bodies.

And Elizabeth sang…

Named me blessed.

Myself, and the babe
I bore, His presence
So alive in me
That it blazed
From my womb
To Elizabeth's:

Shone before the child
Who dwelt
In its shadows.

I praised The Lord my God
As though my soul
Had wings,
On fire with the mystery
Of our humble lives
And at their heart
My promised child,

Greater than us all
In His hidden smallness.

Mary in Advent

Luke 1:26-37

I would not hurry him
Though I move slowly,
Awkward as a tree
Almost too small
For its nearly ripened fruit.

I spread out more branches,
My body finding the space
That my heart desires
And I marvel
At the wonder
Of it all.

Afternoons, I nod
Over half-woven linen;
Startle, as he uncurls,
Arches his back,
Re-threads my day.

How could I hurry him?
See how he delights me
With every kick and nudge
Of his beautiful feet.

Will they be miniatures
Of my own?

He will come
When time comes together
In my woman's time
And his baby head breaks
The warm secret waters.

Then I shall count each hour
Until he lies
Across my breast,
Rosy mouth ready
To waken the earth!

Nativity

Luke 2; 6-19

I dreamt a morning
Crisp as linen;
Sunburst
Of birdsong
And women's hands.

Instead,
A cave's tilted shadows
And oxen's hot breath.
Shepherds, angel-dazed
From their midnight fields
Who knelt in adoration,
Described a silver sky
Alight with praise
For my newborn son.

I treasured their words,
Locked them in my heart.

Pondered, too,
The mystery
Of his helplessness,
The wonder
Of his need;

Lifted him
To my breast
As his fledgling mouth
Wailed
For my body's milk,
My arms' tireless nesting.

With Joseph

Matthew 1 & 2 and Luke 2

He slept, most
Of the journey,
Wrapped tightly
Against my heart
For we travelled by night,
Anxious to stay unseen.
But when he did awake
(His eyes still that
Perfect baby blue)
And looked up
Into our faces
He was our star,
Our unfailing hope.

And months later
After I had bathed him,
Dried his downy little head
I thought all at once
He is my Peace.
I have given birth
To the Prince
Of Peace...

I was glad, then,
To sit with Joseph
At my side; share
The joy and confusion
Of this anointed parenthood.

Joseph, my gentle spouse,
Who knew how it was
To see our newborn son
Adored by shepherds;
Rich men from the East;
Prophets in the Temple.

Joseph, whose dreams
Were disturbed by angels.

He obeyed their commands:
Let sacred messages
Shape our future,

Weave themselves daily
Through our simple tasks
As though no cloud
Divided Heaven and earth.

John's Baptism

Matthew 3:13-17 & Luke 1 39-45

Elizabeth's son
And mine, together
At the river's edge,
John leading the way
As he had
All those years ago
When his mother's hands
Flew to the vastness
Beneath her gown
And a joyful greeting
Danced from her lips.

Elizabeth's son,
Immersing mine
In the river's stillness.

I watch his head rise,
Hair pasted down
All dark and sticky,
Mouth gasping for breath.

Then the water breaks,
The heavens open
And a dove hovers
Like a quivering star.

*This is my Son, the Beloved,
My favour rests on Him*

Words that feel plucked
From my heart
For I rejoice
In his wisdom;
Call him "my beloved".

But never like this.
Never this anointing
Of fire and kinship

Throbbing through a sky
That almost shatters
Into eggshells.

I have done
All I promised;
Loved and protected him
For thirty shining years:
Prepared him
For the Father's work.

And if there is emptiness;
Anxious days
Of silent endearments?

Oh, Elizabeth,
Sweetly-remembered cousin,
I see clearly
How I am blessed
Even as you proclaimed
When John leaped
In your womb.

Blessed for the fruit I bore;

Ripe, at last,
To be shared
Among so many.

Peter's Walk

Matthew 14:22-33

He was his own light
In that torrential darkness.

No dawn
Ever broke so early
Or shaped itself
Into a flame-white robe
That travelled towards us
On bloated waves.

I yelled with the others
Though sensed it was him
Before I heard his voice.

His greeting unnerved me.

I AM WHO I AM...

Always assumed
But never quite stated.

Until now.

Without warning.

Hot anxious words
Bubbled to my lips,
My thoughts in chaos
After a day when
He blessed five loaves
And fed a multitude.

Oh, I loved him,
Trusted him,
Had left everything
To be with him.

But these miracles
That changed the laws
Of nature....

This revelation
Of who he was
As he tamed a sea
I no longer knew.

I needed to reach
Under his skin,
Walk as he had walked
On unresisting water.

So I strode out
Towards the God
Of Abraham and Isaac
And Jacob...

Until the wind
Trapped my feet.

The treacherous wind
That snatched up boats
And dropped them
Down again
In splintered pieces.

He held out his hands
And I buckled
Into his arms.

A cry echoed
Across the waves:

My heart's reply,
Wiser than
The wanderings
Of my dizzy head.

The Woman Who Was A Sinner

Luke 7:36-50

I came with perfume
To honour and delight him;
Sold all my jewellery
For the finest nard,
Knelt ready with my jar.

But at the music
Of his voice
I became once more
That bedraggled,
Broken- winged bird
He had pitied and saved.

I wept.
Half a lifetime
Of tears, set free
From the well
Of my being.

A fierce cleansing
Yet he did not flinch:
Knew all there was
Of me; had taken
Every scarlet sin
And laid it
Against his breast.

A poor exchange,
My tear stains
For his forgiveness….
So I spread out my hair,
Dried his beautiful
Blameless feet
With those glossy curls
Men once teased
Around their fingers.

My womanhood's glory
And truly my own, now,
To offer or refuse.

The Women Who Followed Jesus

Luke 8:1-3

We heard how she waited
At the Pharisee's house,
Lavished tears and ointment
Upon his feet
Then swabbed them
With her unbound hair.

We shed our own tears
At such courage;
Recalled the first time
We had met him...

Heard him preach
And jostled through the crowd
To seek his face.

The Rabbi from Nazareth
Who ignored no woman
Or wide-eyed child.

Each encounter different,
As we were
From one another.

But we all rejoiced
In a setting-free:
Shadows lifted
From half-hidden worlds
Of barrenness, widowhood,
Moods that swung
With the stormy tide.

We opened our hearts
Like flowers to the sun.

And though we brought no perfume
Sealed in alabaster jars
We seemed to grow fragrant
In his presence,

His love the perfect balm
Poured out in abundance,
His words the wellspring
Of our loyal sisterhood
That followed him and his Disciples
From town to town;
Made sure they had meals
And freshly- laundered clothes.

We faced hostile stares,
Braved market-place gossip.

Others whispered
That he favoured us
Over his own dear Mother.

This, we knew, was false,
Though we felt closer to him
Than servants, even friends:

Were more his family
Than we truly understood.

Martha's Part

Luke 10:38-42

I am serving the meal
For Jesus and his Disciples.
He glances up at me
And smiles.
All is well.
This is where I belong,
Keeping house
For Lazarus and Mary,
Sharing our table
With neighbours and friends.

And while I work
I pray silently
To God our Father,
Offer him thanks
For His daily provision.

The room is warm
With laughter,
Everyone content.

I nod, satisfied...

It was always my touch
That set the day in motion,
Kept our family together.

Mary tried to help,
A scowl on her pretty face
As she untangled wool
Or burnt a second batch
Of morning's bread.

It never really mattered.

Until we noticed
How Jesus had changed;
Watched the flame

Of his being
Blaze into a fire.

They were drawn-
Mary and Lazarus-
More eagerly
Than moths at twilight.

I could not follow;
Stay for hours
As though time
Meant nothing.

I had work to do,
A house to run....

And in my loneliness
Let it rule my heart.

One thundery evening
When the more I bustled
The less I did
Envy spurted from my lips
Like sour milk.

He chided me.
Gently enough,
But tears came later
In great ugly gulps.

Because I loved him too
And wanted the peace
He had given
My wayward young sister.

Because I loved him too
And he might never know......

I slip back unnoticed
And join the others,
Tuck my arm
Around Mary's waist.
The room is hushed

While the Master
Explains a parable.

He has shown me
The better part;
Opened a pathway
Through my desert
Of self-reliance.

I am learning
To let go:
Trust in his promise
Of the Father's care.

Peter's Feet

After the painting by Sieger Koder

John 13:1-17

He washed my feet.

Began with the others
And when it was my turn
I would have stopped him;
Blustered on
As I usually did…

*Then why just
My feet, Master?*

But he had his way
As he always did
And I took the bowl.

Only after Calvary
(And now, as I wait
For my own death)
Could I remember
The slope
Of his spine,

His back
Bent so low
I sat above him,

My head ledged
Across his neck,
One hand upon
His shoulder blade

Locked closer
Than close friends.

Oh, soft lapping
Of summer tide,
His hands a paddle

Of leaves.

And reflected
In the water

My feet
And everyone's dust

All mingled
With the sweetness
Of his face.

Peter at Gethsemane

Mark 14:32-42

John blamed the wine:
Stronger, more potent
Than usual.

We were half dead
With drowsiness.

No ordinary Passover,
This …

I had already grappled
To make sense
Of his strange
Sad words….

Watched them slither away
Like fish through torn nets.

And when he repeated
"Betrayal" I was lost.
Spoke for the others,
Protested for myself:

To love him once
Was to love forever.

He took us
Into the olive grove,
Asked us to wait;
Stay awake
While he prayed alone.

We fought sleep
And heady wine.

Trees swayed, moaned,
Hissed my name.

A wind gathered pace,
Began to buffet me,
Shake me....

Only his voice
In my ear,
His arm
Across my shoulder.

My Lord,
On his knees
In the grass,
Desperate for help
Like a drowning man
And I offered no hand
To pull him free.

My eyelids drooped:
I let them close.

Knew, then, I had
Drunk the cup
Of his grief
And could drink
No more,

Could not watch
As it ran crimson
Through the night.

Peter's Denial

Luke 22; 54-62

A numbness,
Sitting there
In the courtyard
Hunched
Over the fire,

Wanting to sit there
Forever,
Frozen in time
While the world
Carried on around me
And me in it
Somewhere

As though nothing
Had ever happened.

A simple fisherman
From Galilee.

Why should that
Mark me out?

Numbness my refuge
Until that silly
Plangent bird
Crowed twice
And He came
From the High Priest's house.

My Master,
Flanked by guards.

If He'd called
In reproach
I'd have bluffed my way
To Hell.

But his look

Beckoned me
Into the cradle
Of His heart.

The look
That always undid me.

I had to run
From such perfect love,
Fall on my face
In the dust.

I had to die
A thousand deaths,
Empty vows unmasked.

I had to weep
Until my head throbbed
For another, gentler night
When he walked towards me
On indigo waves,

Arms outstretched
To carry my fear.

At the foot of the Cross

cf.John 19: 25-27

They shall not have it,
They shall not have his robe.....

Words shrivel within me,
My voice snatched by grief
Like a leaf in the wind.

They have thrown their dice,
Gamble for the robe
I wove so lovingly
(Though I would have
Clothed them, too,
Had they asked)

Nothing spares my pain.
This is my time
As well as his:
Snow and ice
In the marrow
Of my soul;
The piercing sorrow
Foretold by Simeon
When he cradled
My fragrant babe
And old, tired eyes
Grew young.

Did you see him,
Gentle prophet?
My firstborn son,
Naked and bruised once more
But nailed to a broken tree?

"Child, child" I cried,
"My little sparrow
What have they done to you?"

But he answered to a love

Greater, even, than mine.

I could not lullaby
His anguish
Nor bathe his wounds;

Could only stand and pray
With those who wept
For us both.

They are bringing him
Down, now;
Carry him towards me.

I hold out my arms.

Simeon, this sword
Will stop my heart.

Its blade comes again.

Hear it thud,
Dark and deep
Between my ribs.

The Weeping Women

Luke 23; 27-31

If you command it,
We will weep
For ourselves.

But let it be
With each other
And for each other:
Together, hand in hand,
United in the grief
That only woman know.....

Babies who come too quickly
Or are lost in a heartbeat.
Children taken by fevers
We would gladly have borne
(Anything, but to rock them,
 Pretend they only sleep.)

Innocent daughters
And beautiful blameless sons
Imprisoned, tortured,
Killed in the name
Of justice...

This we share
And more.

But let it be
As we follow you
On your dusty, stumbling way.

For you are our
Freedom and fulfilment:
You, Creator, who never shunned
Our bodies' ebb and flow
But healed its sickness,
Forgave its sin.

You, Master, who exalted
Our humble state:
Treasured our hearts' tenderness,
Wooed our minds' tenacity.

This you have done
And more.

We will weep, then,
As we walk arm in arm
With Veronica
And Mary of Magdala
And Mary your Mother.

Let us stand
Beneath your Cross
In patient faith
While your precious blood
Seals our small deaths
Onto yours;

Pours new life
Into the bare tree,
The broken wood.

The women at the tomb

Luke 24; 1-11

Was this our *"thank you"*:
To be the first to know?

We never asked for praise
Nor expected it.

His smile was enough.

Yet angels greeted us
Before Peter; James;
The Beloved Disciple.

Such dazzled fear,
Such dizzy amazement.
Such joy, such relief,
Such certainty!

We ran with fire in our feet
To reveal the news
Though nothing we glowed with
Could wake their souls' dark night,
Open their shuttered despair.

Only He could do that.

We grieved no less
Than His Disciples…

But time had few spaces
To let us mourn.

Always our way,
To weep or rejoice
Within our hearts
While we shopped, cooked;
Scrubbed grass-stained robes
Or soothed dusty throats.

Then while they slept
And the wood burned low
We shared miracles, mysteries;
Re-told how He rescued us
With His pure and startling love.

Yes, this was our blessing
As we brought oils and spices:

Skilled at dignifying death
But entrusted instead
With death become life
And its endless proclamation.

Peter And The Lord's Hands

His hands
Were always beautiful.

I raged
When I heard
How they were torn;
Half expected my guilt
And bitter grief
To make them whole.

I had seen them
So often, ready
To bless, heal:

Wash our calloused feet
With a slow tenderness.

Anointed hands, fragrant
With olive and cedar
Yet toughened by his trade.

Hands that held me upright
On fickle waves.

I crowded with the others
When he returned,
Anxious to examine, probe,
Make certain.

I touched his palms:
Met a sobbing emptiness.

Master, Master,
You could have covered
These marks, made the skin
Grow back again...

I simmered
But did not speak.

He knew, of course,
Smiled in his special way.

Smiled again at my silence
When dawn spilled like wine
Into a listless Galilee
And he cooked breakfast
On the shore.

His palms glistened,
Almost in the fire.

Smoke stung my eyes
As he took the bread,
Shared it among us.

Memories surfaced
Through my tears' haze…

Another place, another meal.

And forgiveness
Broke from his wounds,

Rushed like the tide
Across my heart.

The Meeting

I woke before dawn,
Disturbed by insistent light
And a voice
From some long-ago Spring.

I thought it was the angel
Who had greeted me
At Nazareth;
Stumbled across the room
To a wide open door…

Then I knew.

Clothed in the softest
Of blue-white
Shimmering brightness.

"Jesus?
Jesus my son?"

He smiled
As only he could smile.

I have come to you first
My mother, my love

I found a robe;
One I'd darned yesterday
Ready for John;
Fetched some wine,
Bustled about with food
Until he took me gently
By the shoulders,
Sat me at the table.

He ate the corner
Of last night's bread.
It smelled fresh, warm.

I feasted on his face;

Traced his features,
Smoothed out his hair…

Will you stay with my friends
Now and through the ages?
Be there, while they wait
For my Spirit?

Your love will comfort them,
Your prayer will steady them.
Will you be their Mother
As you are mine and John's?

I whispered that I would
And kissed his hands;
Held them against my face:

Against my ageing
Unpierced skin.

Peter's Answer

John 21:15-23

Did he ask
For his own heart's sake,
One friend to another?

He called me
By my birth name,
My old name:
Sudden reassurance
In the morning's turmoil.

I needed to answer
Again
     Again
Again

Discover that love
Was greater than
Injured pride;
Let thorn-pricks
Of sorry tears
Scald my cheeks.

Fire and cloud
Spluttered and swirled.

(A cock crowed
The last time,
Curdled the air.)

Now, the lake's
Shush-shush
And his command
To follow.

As though I had never
Followed him before.

I rose at once,
Puzzled by his words
For I stood gladly,
Looked around for John.

He was to remain,
The Master said.

John: a sun's ray
The heavens had lent us
While I......?

Cephas; shepherd;
Fisherman chosen
To trawl
For men's lives.

So I left my boat
And my swollen
Unwashed nets
As though I had never
Left them before;

Hurried across
Sand and stone
To match, stride
For clumsy stride,

The marks
Of his narrow footfall.

Man of Light

Dedicated to His Holiness Pope John Paul II

Inspired by Rosarium Virginis Mariae

Light rippling from your pen
Like sun through frozen water
Stunning the heavy ice,
Melting its stiff unkindness.

Light irresistible,
Light indivisible,

Light
From the Light
Of the World
Cradling your soul,
Bathing your pain,

Re-kindling the smile
In your eyes, on your lips,
As when daybreak discovers
An ancient, stained-glass window;

Glass so fragile
Weathered so long
It holds more
Of the Bright Morning Star
Than its own fading colours.

Towards The End

In Memoriam Pope John Paul 11 1920-2005

You were still the light
On the hilltop
And our Faith's bright mountain
That nothing could overpower.

Not shaking hands
Nor faltering speech.
Not trembling lips
Nor tired head.
Not bowed, humbled shoulders
Nor legs that had buckled
Under their body's weight
Though once, they guided skis
Down sparkling white slopes.

Not these
Nor any other thing
For light shone through
Even pain's creeping darkness:
Light of the Holy Spirit
That constantly burned
Renewed, outpoured
Into broken earthenware.

Light that was not fully yours;
Light you carried serenely
As Mary carried her child.

Waiting for the Wine

I light a candle
Before your image;
Want to hide my head
In your lap, share
My loneliness and hurt.

Mother who watches,
Mother who listens;
Mother who speaks
To her Blessed Son
As you did, first, at Cana,
Though you sit closer now
Than if I had met you
At the wedding feast.

Mother of Mercy,
Your love untied
From place and time
When you stood
Beneath the Cross;
Let John become your son
And a people yet unborn
Your wayward children.

I kneel at your altar,
Peace falling about me
And your smile
Seems to broaden,

My gaze following yours
To greet the infant
In your arms:
The One who stills
Wind and waves.

You hold him towards me,
Urge me to seek his face…
Child become man,
Who drank deep

Of his Father's cup.

Word become flesh
Who gives his life
Again and again:

The broken bread,

The unmeasured wine

Transformed by his Spirit
Into the blood
Of my healing.

Easter Vigil

Wood
Of the tree
Is burning,

Burning,

Length
Of the hours
Is turning,

Turning
From sorrow
To joy

For the Flower
Is awoken,
Stone hearts
Are flesh,

A night-wind
Blows where it will
And sparks are escaping,
Showering at our feet.

We step back,
We who have watched
The Paschal Candle
Dipped in the swirling blaze;

Sanctified, sealed,
Become the named
And wounded light
For all who plunge
To death with Him,
Rise in His Spirit.

But we are caught already:
We, who are not
The unquenchable Light

But beloved children
Of the Light,
Our own small tapers
Lit from a single flame
Then each from the other.

Lamps in a sea
Of darkness
As we slowly move;

Follow the beeswax pillar
Through parted doors.

Eucharist

Twilight,
And I look back
Upon my day.

The hoovered bedrooms
And peeled potatoes;
The hand-written letter
And neighbourly smile.

Familiar litany
Of littleness; routine
Of almost-nothingness.

Except that you, Jesus,
Are its Beginning
And End;
Morning Star
Who led me
From my soul's secret room
To another meeting place
Where gifts were prepared
On the altar.

I knelt before the Father;
Gathered the grains
Of my housework;

Retrieved the trails
Of my fatigue.

Waited,
While the gifts
Were offered.

Watched,
While the unseen Spirit
United my mundane acts
To your perfect sacrifice;
Accepted all I had,

Not just then
But now, as twilight
Slides into evening,

Your presence beyond
Space and time,

Your Body and Blood
Still redeeming the day
I look back upon;

Fold into Mystery.

Post Communion

I have everything
I need.

I am complete;
Held in your care
Like a hand
In a custom-made glove.

I kneel
In silent worship,
Haloed by
Summer-evening sun
As it shimmers
Through stained glass,
Restores the forgotten Saints.

Soon, the Priest
Will dismiss us all
And I cannot cling
To this serenity
Like gentle Winifrede
In her blue crystal robe;

Find a place at her side,
Pray beyond nightfall
In hushed seclusion.

I must go into the world
And proclaim your truth;
Carry no white-gold lily
Plucked from Winifrede's grasp

But the peace you bequeath,
The love that bears witness:

Your living body
Alight within my own.

Adoration of the Blessed Sacrament

You still me
With your beauty

When I rush in
From the street
And kneel
In your presence
And the noise
Of buses and cars
Ebbs swiftly
Into the distance
And my unruly breath
Slows

To the beat

Of your heart.

Not my will
But yours.
Not my power
But yours
Pulling me
Into your orbit,

Revealing the dark
And dusty corners
Of my soul.

Then,
As a mother
To her child,
You kiss my blotchy
Tear-stained face,

Cleanse it
With your forgiveness,

Bathe it

In your healing,

Show me
Something new
In the mirror
Of your love.

Lamb

cf. John 1: 29-35

How vulnerable
You are.
How small.

Nothing was ever
More frail
And unprotected
Than this fragment
Of wafer

Light as
A falling leaf.

Dependent
On the hand
That holds you
And on that hand's
Devotion.

Nothing was ever
So fine and pure.

John saw
Where the Spirit
Came to rest
And knew you, then;
Called out your name
As you walked by.

Time for his disciples
To follow you,
Everything set in place
For a love
That would be
Ground like wheat;

Return to life

And be broken again
By hands
That lift you;

Place you
In my cupped
And waiting palm.

The Triumph

I look upon
All that demeans;

God's anointed Son
Pinned against wood
As wood is
To itself.

Flesh and bone
Hammered to wood.

Hands and feet
Nailed to wood.

His body naked
But for a loin cloth,

His head bowed
Beneath its
Tangled crown,

His arms outstretched
As though
They would snap.

I look upon
The Cross
And I see love
Without pride
Or self-will;

A hidden heart
Throbbing
With boundless mercy,

Struggling to beat,

Ceasing to beat….

Waiting for a lance
To release
Water and blood:

Open the gateway
To our souls' redemption.

Father

In Memoriam Patrick Cooper 1917-1965

"Too frail"
Lamented my Gran,
*"To lift even
His little finger."*

It was a few days
Before you died.

I never spoke
Of what happened:

How I dawdled
Behind the others
After we left the ward,
Peered through a window
To glimpse you again.

You craned forward
On your pillows
And waved:
Firmly, cheerfully.

I waved back
And we smiled,
As though part
Of some beautiful
Hallowed secret.

I rebelled, soon,
Against beliefs
You had cherished;

Locked them away
Like outgrown toys
Until my own child's exile
Turned me home.

I saw, then,
How your prayers
Had pursued me
Through college,
Marriage, motherhood,
While the icon
Of your caring face,
And impossible wave
Tugged at the long
Long cord
That wound back
To the Father's heart.

I'm sure
You watched, Dad,
When He cloaked me
In His forgiveness.

I like to think
You smiled:

Lifted your hand
To wave.

Ben

For Ben, Kathy and Jimmy, my wonderful grandchildren

The year was only
Three days old
When your coming
Changed it forever.

Hours after your birth,
Your face translucent
With perfect newness,
We feel we have
Always known you.

We devour
The first photographs;
Marvel at how you lie,
Cosied in white
Across your mother's breast,
One tiny paw
Tucked against her throat.

Her hand curves
Around your smallness.

She is your certainty;
The fragrance you recognize
From that other world
Where you floated
And back-flipped,
Did forward rolls
And sucked your thumb,
An immortal soul within you
Even before
Your toes unwebbed
And your fingers danced.

Impossible not to think
Of another baby
Who shared his Mother's womb:

59

Became flesh
As man and child,
Embryo and foetus;
Hiccupped and back-flipped
And prayed to the Father
For our redemption.

Fresh from the space
He has sanctified,
Your likeness stills us
Into quiet reverence.

****

She places you
On my lap
And smiles.
My younger daughter
With her firstborn.

She knows I have
Waited weeks for this.

I am ready;
Have waited a lifetime.

I kiss your head,
Transfer you
To my shoulder's
Special niche
Where I nursed your cousins.

You greet me
With two fat burps
And giant posset
On my favourite blouse
And we are best friends;
Understand each other,
You and I.

You close your eyes
And burrow down.

I listen to every squeak

And contented sigh;
Feel the rise and fall
Of your chest
As you warm my body
With your own,
Smooth my heart's
Jagged edges.

And while the others
Chat, drink their tea,
You draw me close
To the One
You dream about;

Sleep sweetly
And profoundly
In his Incarnate
Newborn image.

Christmas Meditation

Isaiah 11; 1-9

At the old earth's dying
A little child waits
To make all things new.

Child who is
And was
And always will be
Yet grew to fruition
In his mother's womb.

He will bring
Endless day

Endless day

With light more radiant
Than sun or moon.

And I have heard
Choirs of angels
Join the cry
Of my heart;
Must hurry
From my soul's
Dry season
To find a manger
Filled with straw
Where he lies,
White-swaddled and shining
At his Mother's side.

Oh blessed Babe
You captivate me!

Your littleness
Calms me.

Your beauty
Anoints me.

And as you wake,
Light that is love
Already kindles
In your birth-blue eyes,

Concealing nothing
Of what I am,

Revealing the promise
Of all I shall be.

Printed in Great Britain
by Amazon

29644706R00038